T0124565

A is for **A**manda Nunes. As the only fighter in UFC history – male or female – to hold and defend two division championship titles concurrently, this Brazilian beast is undoubtedly the greatest female mixed martial artist of all time. All hail, the legendary Lioness!

B is for **B**.J. Penn. Earning his BJJ black belt in just three years, The Prodigy was respected for his readiness to fight any opponent regardless of weight class. The two-division champ is both a welterweight and lightweight title holder. Legend!

**C is for Daniel Cormier.
With championship titles in
both the UFC and Strikeforce,
DC is a respected MMA
veteran. Epically losing to only
two fighters in his entire UFC
career – Jon Jones and Stipe
Miocic – he retired a two-
division legend of the sport.**

D is for **D**emetrious Johnson. Winning the inaugural UFC flyweight championship title and defending it a record-making 11 times, Mighty Mouse is one of the greatest pound-for-pound mixed martial artists of all time. His Mighty Wiz Bar submission was just legendary!

E is for Fedor **E**melianenko. He casually showed up wearing his trademark sweater, but once his fights began, this stoic Russian exploded into a punishing ground-and-pound warrior – making The Last Emperor the greatest Pride heavy-weight champion of all time.

F is for Forrest Griffin.
His famous bout with Stephan Bonnar was Dana White's "most important fight in UFC history," and brought MMA back into the mainstream. Showing true grit and heart, Griffin later defeated 'Rampage' Jackson to claim the light heavyweight title.

G is for Royce **G**racie. At just 180 pounds, the Godfather of MMA rocked the world of combat sports when he won the open-weight tournament-style UFC 1 in 1993! He brought Gracie Jiu-Jitsu to the mainstream and forever revolutionized the world of mixed martial arts. Legend!

H is for Matt **H**ughes. Famous for his ground-and-pound farm boy strength, this American two-time UFC welterweight champion dominated his division. His trilogy bouts with GSP and B.J. Penn, as well as catch-weight fight against legend Royce Gracie, cemented his status as an MMA great.

I is for Israel Adesanya. A former professional kickboxer, this Nigerian-born Kiwi has become an undisputed UFC force of nature, delivering some legendary highlight-reel knockouts. The Last Style-bender bagged his first UFC middleweight championship within only two years of joining the organization.

J is for **J**on Jones. As methodical as he is athletic, this controversial record-holding G.O.A.T. has found no opponent too challenging for him. Bones has wiped out generations of light heavyweight legends with calculated game plans and devastating elbows – and he's not done yet!

K is for **K**en Shamrock. The World's Most Dangerous Man was one of MMA's pioneers alongside fellow legend Royce Gracie. Crowned the King of Pancrase, Shamrock was the first foreign MMA champion in Japan and was the UFC's first Superfight sensation.

L is for Chuck Liddell. One of the sport's most popular light heavyweights, The Iceman was revered for his ferocity and power. His legendary rivalries with Tito Ortiz and Randy Couture in the early 2000s brought MMA into the mainstream of American sport and entertainment.

M is for Conor McGregor. He's 'The Notorious' Irish showman, the original champ-champ, the biggest box office sensation the sport has ever seen. His 13-second knockout of José Aldo and world-stopping Money Fight with G.O.A.T boxer Floyd Mayweather will go down in the history books!

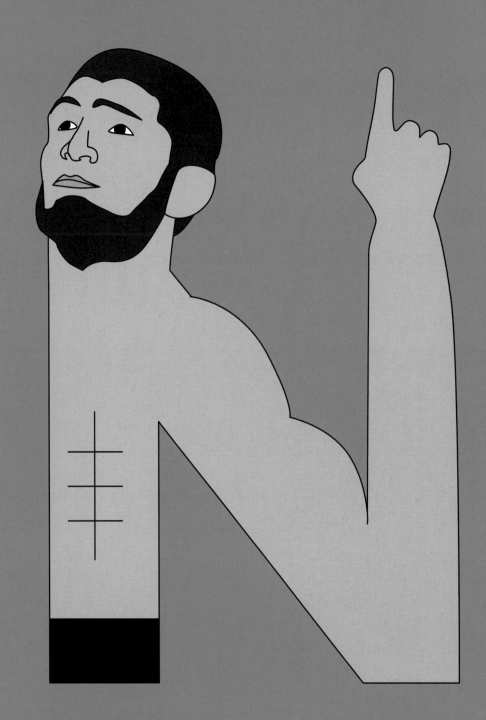

N is for Khabib **N**urmagomedov. Hailing from the harsh Russian mountains of Dagestan, The Eagle trained under the tutelage of his legendary father Abdulmanap. Wrestling bears as a child, he developed the most ferocious and dominating wrestling style the sport has ever seen!

Oo

O is for Tito **O**rtiz. The Huntington Beach Bad Boy was the original smack-talking showman of the UFC, starting the legendary rivalry with Chuck Liddell that launched the sport into the mainstream. He defended his light heavyweight crown a then-record five times.

P is for Georges St-Pierre. This French Canadian two-division welterweight and middleweight champ not only avenged his two UFC career losses, but also triumphantly won the rematches by stoppage. GSP retired in 2019 as one of the undisputed best fighters of all time.

Qq

Q is for **Q**uinton Jackson. With his eccentric howls, thundering striking power and legendary rivalries with Chuck Liddell and Wanderlei Silva, Rampage is one of MMA's superstars, entertaining audiences in the cage as well as in movies and on TV.

R is for **R**onda Rousey. Single-handedly convincing Dana White to create a UFC women's division, Rowdy elevated women not only in MMA, but everywhere. Olympic Judo bronze medalist, UFC Hall of Famer, WWE champ — she's truly "one of the defining athletes of the 21st century."

S is for Anderson Silva. Undeniably one of the greatest mixed martial artists of all time, this middleweight legend has delivered some of the UFC's most iconic knockouts and submissions. The Spider also holds the UFC record for the longest title reign (2,457 days)!

T is for Henry 'Triple C' Cejudo. Love him or hate him, the King of Cringe is a triple champion, winning an Olympic wrestling gold medal, defeating the great Demetrious Johnson for the UFC flyweight belt, and capturing the bantamweight title at the same time.

U is for **U**rijah Faber. Putting 145-pound fighters on the map, The California Kid defended his WEC featherweight title five times. Athletic, enduring and all-round nice guy, he is one of the most revered lightweight fighters in MMA history.

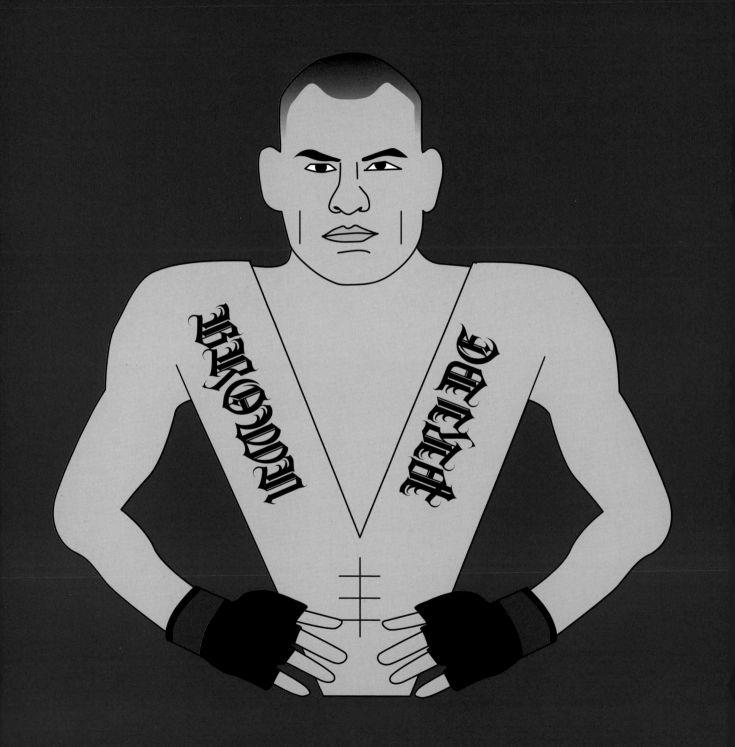

Vv

V is for Cain Velasquez. Constantly either striking or shooting for a takedown, Cardio Cain is a formidable opponent. His famous first-round TKO win over Brock Lesnar earned him Knockout of the Night honors and his first UFC heavyweight title.

W is for **W**anderlei Silva. True to his Chute Boxe training, Silva was a savage in the cage. From his chilling stare downs to his knockout power and brilliance in the Thai clinch, The Axe Murderer was a Pride middleweight legend!

X is for Randy 'Xtreme' Couture. With his own chain of Xtreme Couture gyms, he defied age to become the oldest ever UFC world champion at 46. An international Greco-Roman competitor, former U.S. Army sergeant and now Hollywood actor, The Natural is a true MMA icon.

Y is for Yoel Romero.
This Cuban warrior and
Olympic wrestling Silver
medalist is one of the most
athletic fighters in the sport.
Even in his 40s, Soldier of
God stuns with his spinning
strikes, skillful takedowns
and explosive knockouts.

Zz

Z is for Weili **Z**hang.
After a stellar career in China as a Kunlun strawweight champion and Top FC titleholder, she exploded onto the UFC scene with Magnum force and became China's first ever UFC champ. What a legend!

The ever-expanding legendary library

EXPLORE THESE LEGENDARY ALPHABETS & MORE AT WWW.ALPHABETLEGENDS.COM